Passive Income Stream Generator

I0480317

Top 10 Ways to Financial Freedom

Copyright 2017 by C.J. ELLIOTT - All rights reserved.

The follow eBook is reproduced below with the goal of providing information that is as accurate and reliable as possible. Regardless, purchasing this eBook can be seen as consent to the fact that both the publisher and the author of this book are in no way experts on the topics discussed within and that any recommendations or suggestions that are made herein are for entertainment purposes only. Professionals should be consulted as needed prior to undertaking any of the action endorsed herein.

This declaration is deemed fair and valid by both the American Bar Association and the Committee of Publishers Association and is legally binding throughout the United States.

Furthermore, the transmission, duplication or reproduction of any of the following work including specific information will be considered an illegal act irrespective of if it is done electronically or in print. This extends to creating a secondary or tertiary copy of the work or a recorded copy and is only allowed with express written consent from the Publisher. All additional right reserved.

The information in the following pages is broadly considered to be a truthful and accurate account of facts and as such any inattention, use or misuse of the information in question by the reader will render any resulting actions solely under their purview. There are no scenarios in which the publisher or the original author of this work can be in any fashion deemed liable for any hardship or damages that may befall them after undertaking information described herein.

Additionally, the information in the following pages is intended only for informational purposes and should thus be thought of as universal. As befitting its nature, it is presented without assurance regarding its prolonged validity or interim quality. Trademarks that are mentioned are done without written consent and can in no way be considered an endorsement from the trademark holder.

Introduction

Congratulations on downloading Passive Income Stream Generator: Top 10 Ways to Financial Freedom and thank you for doing so. It doesn't matter if you are looking for an escape from your 9-to-5 or looking for a way to save for retirement, passive income is the answer. It definitely takes more than wanting it to make it happen, however, which is why so many people give up before they have seen a single red cent.

Luckily, the following chapters will discuss everything you need to know to start generating real results from a wide variety of passive income streams, and also explain how you can stick with them in order to see the best results in the shortest period of time possible. First, you will learn how to generate passive income from traditional methods like investing in rental properties or the stock market. Then you will learn about a variety of different online options including running an online business, affiliate marketing, retail arbitrage, creating digital content, authoring eBooks, selling stock photos and advertising on an Instagram account.

While all of these options are guaranteed to generate passive income in the long term, it is important to keep in mind that it won't happen overnight. Generating a passive income stream takes hard work and dedication up front, so that you can enjoy the fruits of your labors early on. If you are looking for a get rich quick scheme, you are better off saving yourself some time and looking elsewhere instead. If you stick with them, however, you have the potential to make up to thousands of dollars a month with little or no additional effort, you just need to stick with it.

There are plenty of books on this subject on the market, thanks again for choosing this one! Every effort was made to ensure it is full of as much useful information as possible, please enjoy!

Chapter 1: Real Estate

When it comes to passive income, there are few more reliable means than investing in real estate for the purposes of renting it out, after all as Mark Twain once observed, they aren't making any more land. However, while there will always be some property out there that you can make a profit on, it is going to take a significant financial investment up front in order to generate the best return on your investment. If you can manage to pull it off, however, it will reliably generate a return on investment that surpasses practically any other investment strategy while building your portfolio at the same time.

As actively managing both tenants and the upkeep on your rental properties isn't exactly passive, if you decide to go down this route then you are going to want to look into finding a property management company to take care of your rental property for you. This, in turn, limits you primarily to condos or apartment complexes as a majority of property management companies aren't going to be interested in managing single, single family properties. While this will naturally mean a decrease in your profits, it will mean significantly less work as well.

Condominium: Purchasing a condominium is a great choice for new real estate owners as it automatically comes with a property management team in place. Additionally, they are typically going to be a good deal cheaper than other types of property. Furthermore, you will typically attract younger, upwardly mobile tenants who will treat the property well and have little trouble paying the rent on time. On the other hand, you are likely to make less overall with them, both because the rent is typically going to be less than other property types and also because you are going to make less from appreciation as the value of condos rise more slowly than single family homes.

Small apartment complexes: Small apartment complexes are another good type of starter rental property as their size means you won't have to take on too much all at once. Additionally, if the property doesn't already have a contract with an existing property management company you can often find someone to live on site and provide these services in exchange for free housing. Additionally, they are often considered quite reliable as you will have several different people paying rent all at once which means it is unlikely they will all be unable or unwilling to pay at all at the same time.

The biggest downside to these types of properties is that your future tenant prospects are typically limited by the type of individuals who currently live there. If the previous landlord did their due diligence and found quality tenants then you are golden, if they rented to questionable individuals then you will have trouble attracting respectable tenants until the others move out.

Finding the right property: When it comes to choosing the right property for you, the first thing you are going to need to do is to consider various neighborhoods that look promising for rental properties based on local conditions. This means looking for neighborhoods that have access to amenities that renters would be interested that are also close to areas that offer a wide range of jobs. As you are going to most likely be looking to attract single individuals instead of families, amenities like local nightlife and easy access to public transportation.

Once you have determined what you are looking for, you are going to want to do some leg work and visit potential neighborhoods both during the day and at night in order to ensure the neighborhood doesn't change dramatically between the two. You should also make a point of talking to current renters in the area to see what they think of it as a whole. Renters will always give you a more honest response as they have no real stake in the area.

You will also want to do your research and determine what the property tax in the area is like when compared to the area as a whole. It is important to research exactly where you are looking as property taxes can vary dramatically, even in neighborhoods that are right next to one another.

Confirming the right rental price: Once you find a property that you are interested in, the next thing you are going to want to do is run the numbers and ensure that it is legitimately going to be worth your time and effort to move forward based on the potential return. This means you are going to want to look at what other rents in the area are like before factoring in anything that makes your property unique, and thus worth more or less than the average. With that number in mind you will then need to factor in the cost you will pay for insurance, your loan payment, taxes and property management fees and then subtract all of that from the amount you will pay for rent.

The amount that is left over from this exercise is going to be what you can expect to make each month on rent. You are going to also want to assume that the property is going to sit empty for at least one month each year to account for periods where a renter has moved out and another has yet to move in. From there, you will then need to subtract out another 10 percent to account for things like missed payments and repairs that you will have to make each year. If the amount left over seems like it would be worth your time then you know you have a property that is worth moving forward with.

Move forward with a plan: Before you start looking at properties you are going to need to have a clear idea what type of loan you will qualify for, what your cash on hand is looking like and if you are going to be looking into hard money or dealer financing loans. Moving forward with a clear plan in mind will make it easier to limit your search to reasonable properties and make it easier for you to negotiate successfully once you have found something that works for you.

Chapter 2: Financial Investing

Choosing to invest in stocks that pay out dividends is a great way to generate a passive income stream. Although it is somewhat riskier than trading stocks as you have to hold the stocks you choose for a greater period of time in order to turn a profit. A dividend is paid out by the company in question to its shareholders on a set schedule and is based on the amount of profit the company has seen over a given period of time. Dividends can come in the form of stock, cash or even property, though this last is less common. Stable companies whose stock does not tend to move much offer dividends as a way to retain, entice and reward shareholders.

As an added benefit, as most dividend paying stocks come from companies that are financially stable, their stock price tends to rise in the long run which means an increase in the dividend payments over time. A company that pays consistently improving dividends is typically going to be a firm that is financially healthy and generates a consistent cash flow. These types of companies are typically extremely stable which means their stock prices are going to be less volatile than the market as a whole. This means that they are typically going to be lower risk than companies that have more volatile price movements, though the potential for holding onto their stock is going to be lower as well.

Another benefit of dividends is the potential to reinvest them back into the dividend producing company, leading to even greater returns in the long run. Many dividend producing companies allow their shareholders to take their payouts in the form of additional shares of stock in the company which is a great choice if you are looking to generate passive income in the long term as it means future payments are going to be even larger when you are ready to capitalize on them.

Dividend investing rules

Finding success with dividend investing isn't rocket science, but it does require an understanding of a handful of basic rules which are outlined below.

Quality supersedes quantity: Perhaps the most important consideration when it comes to choosing stocks with the goal of dividend investment in mind is the rate of dividend yield. Simply put, the greater the yield, the higher the return. However, the numbers can be surprisingly deceptive if you don't know what you are looking for. Specifically, this means you are going to want to make sure that a given company's current payout level is in line with what they have paid out in the past as unsustainable payout levels means there is a chance that the company could stop paying dividends in the future as they are typically given out at the discretion of the company, with no guarantee that they will continue forever.

This means that it is important to look for companies that have a history of paying out regular dividends over the long term as opposed to those that simply offer the highest return at the moment. If you are looking for a buy-and-hold investment then the income generated by low risk dividend stocks will always trump higher amounts in the short term, given a long enough time period.

Avoid new companies: When looking for reliable dividends, you are going to want to stick with those that have earned dividend aristocrat status. Dividend aristocrat status is given out to companies that have given out increasing dividends to stockholders every year, for at least 25 years. These are typically easily recognized brands that always generate a reliable cashflow and have very high odds of continuing to do so in the future.

Be aware of growth potential: In addition to keeping an eye on past returns in comparison to current offerings, it is also important to look to the future potential of a given company before choosing the right dividend-producing stock for you. This is also the main difference between value investing and growth investing. With growth investing, there is less importance placed on where a stock is currently sitting and more emphasis on where it is going to be in the long term. This long-term view will typically give you a much better picture of what its dividend payouts are going to be.

Consider the payout ratio: The dividend payout ratio of a company will often tell you how safe the investment is going to be overall. This ratio measure how much income the company in question is going to retain compared to how much they are currently paying out to their shareholders. Being aware of this number will allow you to tread cautiously around stocks with a high-yield dividend that initially looks promising, but in reality, is taking up a large portion of the given company's profits to generate. In these scenarios, it would only take a small reduction in the company's income stream in order to see the dividend return rate decrease substantially.

Diversify: While concentrating your investment focus on a handful of profitable stocks or a profitable market sector makes sense when the market is strong, it also leaves you vulnerable to market downturns. As this is a long-term strategy then it stands to reason the sector of the market you have chosen to focus on will see this type of downturn a few times before you are ultimately ready to sell off your holdings. This means it is important to diversify the types of stocks you are holding onto in order to ensure that these inevitable downturns impact your passive income stream as little as possible. If dividend payments are then reduced in one area you will have the added security of knowing they are less likely to be reduced across the board which means a majority of your investments will always be safe.

Know when to bow out: While dividend investing is all about taking the long-term view of the stocks you invest in, it is important to keep in mind the difference between taking a long-term view and holding on to a sinking ship. While it is perfectly fine to hold onto the stock of a company that has a history of long-term success who then has a bad year, it is never a good idea to continue holding onto stock in a company that misses its growth goals for more than one year in a row. Missing target growth goals is a sure sign that dividends are going to decrease and the longer you hold onto the related stock, the less you will get for it when you do decide it is time to sell.

Chapter 3: Online Business

If you are looking for a way to start your own online business in a way that will generate relatively passive income, then Fulfillment by Amazon (FBA) is a good place to start. As an FBA member, you find products that you are interested in selling through whatever means you decide upon and then send these items to the nearest Amazon distribution center where they stay until they are sold at which point Amazon ships them off to the buyer without you having to lift a finger. Amazon then also takes on the workload related to dealing with customer service issues as well. In return, they charge you for storage, shipping and take a cut of the profit from the sale. There is also a monthly $40 fee required to utilize the service.

In addition to letting Amazon do a majority of the work, being an FBA member has two other major benefits. First, the items that you sell are automatically eligible for Amazon Prime shipping which means that the millions of Amazon Prime members out there are going to choose your item over a competitor's item even if the competition has a slightly better price. Second, your items will naturally show up higher in the search results which means customers might not even see the competition to begin with.

Maximizing potential

As there is a monthly fee to be an FBA user, it is important to do everything you can to ensure your store makes enough to justify the cost. The following are a list of ways you can do just that.

Choose the right items to sell: First and foremost, even though Amazon is doing most of the work, you are still going to be the face of your store which means you are going to want to do everything in your power to ensure your store rating is as high as possible. This means you are only going to want to stock high quality, reliable items, otherwise customers won't be able to trust that their purchase will be worth their time.

In order to maximize your profits, the first thing you are going to want to do is to download the Amazon Seller Application. This application offers extremely useful functionality in that it allows you to enter the specifics for any product you are hoping to sell and show you how much you will make off of it once all the relevant fees are subtracted from it. It also allows you to determine how many other people are currently selling the same or similar items on Amazon and what they are charging as well. Finally, it shows which versions of a given product, or which brand, is currently the most popular with Amazon customers so you can make your purchasing choices accordingly.

Additionally, before you go ahead and pull the trigger on a given product you are going to want to visit the site CamelCamelCamel.com or one like it. This site provides details relating to how a given product's popularity is trending on Amazon. It shows a detailed graph of the prices that people have been willing to pay for a product over a set period of time which will allow you to determine if a product is growing in popularity (price increasing) or becoming less popular (price decreasing).

Find a niche: While many individuals do fine with stores that sell a wide variety of different products, choosing a niche of products to focus on will allow you to do more accurate research when it comes to determining what types of products to sell. Settling on a niche means you will be able to more easily pinpoint the likes and dislikes of your target audience while also narrowing down ways to find products in that niche for the best prices popular. The best niches are those that have a decent sized following, but are not yet so popular that you are going to be competing with thousands of other FBA members for each and every potential sale.

Take advantage of good deals: While finding a niche will make it easier to find the best products at the best prices in the long run, the number one rule of being success with FBA is that if you find a product that you can make a large profit on, then you should sell it, regardless of what that product happens to be. As such, if you find a product that is currently selling in the real world for one-fourth of the price that it is currently selling for on Amazon then you should buy it as this practically guarantees you are going to net a solid profit once all the fees are taken into account. This is the best way to ensure that this type of passive income stream remains truly passive. When you find these types of deals it is important to have the capital on hand to capitalize on them fully, as it is unlikely they are going to stick around for the long term.

Utilize reward systems: While simply purchasing products cheaply and then selling them for a profit is a perfectly valid strategy, if you want to maximize your benefits from FBA, there is still more you can be doing. First, if you qualify, you are going to want to ensure that you make as many of your purchases as possible with a credit card that generates rewards for purchases. You can then use this card to by gift cards for specific stores and products through sites like GiftCardZen.com. You can then generate money back offers by purchasing items through Ebates.com.

Additionally, you are going to want to keep an eye on websites like RetailMeNot.com and FatWallet.com that offer a variety of coupon codes for things like additional discounts and coupon codes. When purchasing products in the real world you will want to be aware of offers from retail chains such as Kohl's which offer a separate rewards program of their own for repeat customers.

As an example, you could easily purchase a $100 gift card for $90 and then make purchases through Ebates.com to save an additional $3 which is already almost $15 worth of extra profit. You can then save as much as $30 through the judicious use of coupon codes and earn $10 from various rewards programs which drops a $100 purchase down to just $45.

Chapter 4: Affiliate Marketing

If you are already part of an online community that is based around a hobby or interest then you can likely leverage that community into an affiliate marketing-based passive income stream. Affiliate marketing is a type of dedicated advertising where you work with companies or other types of merchants for the purpose of helping them sell their products in return for a cut of the profits of every item sold. This passive income stream requires a bit of work to set up effectively, but it can generate a constant stream of profit when done correctly.

Find a niche: The first thing you are going to need to do is to consider the type of customers you are going to be marketing to. As previously mentioned, if you have a hobby that people are dedicated too then this is a good place to start as you are going to be spending a good deal of time with products related to the niche and having an interest in them beside money making will make the process easier in the long run. If you don't have an idea already in mind then you should choose a hobby for people with a good amount of discretionary income and a steady stream of new products always coming to the market.

Do some research: With a niche in mind, the next thing you are going to want to do is to take some time and visit existing websites where these types of individuals spend their time. You are going to want to consider the types of things that are important to them and the type of products they are likely to buy the most frequently. It is important to take note of their thought processes, the things that are important to them and the slang they use. Sounding like you are one of them is key to making them trust your opinion when you tell them to buy one product over another.

Create a website: In order for this passive income stream to work, you are going to need a blog where you can collect your thoughts and your affiliate marketing articles. When creating your site, keep in mind the types of things you saw on the sites you researched and strive to create a space that members of your niche are going to feel comfortable in. Additionally, you are going to want to create content that is more than just advertisements to ensure that niche members are going to want to get in the habit of visiting your site on the regular.

Affiliate programs: While there are plenty of different companies that offer affiliate programs, the easiest to get started with is Amazon. Once you sign up to be an Amazon affiliate you can choose to sell practically any product you want and they will send you a unique link to that product. Then, whenever a purchase is made through that link, you will receive a commission for the sale. Many new affiliate marketers go straight for the big-ticket items as the commission on these will naturally be higher than with cheaper products.

This is a mistake, however, as it takes much more convincing to get someone to spend several hundred dollars on an item compared to something that is in the fifty-dollar range. When looking for items to sell, quantity is almost always going to trump quality. Another good route to take is to find items that are already discounted on Amazon and let your readers know that if they click on the link you provided they will get a discount on the item in question. Remember, your goal is to close the deal as quickly as possible because even if your review sways a customer in a given direction, if they have to think about the purchase before making it then it is less likely they are going to use your link to do so, which means you won't get credit for your hard work.

Making the sale: When it comes to convincing visitors to your site to purchase things, it is important to do your due diligence with the item in question which means purchasing it for yourself first. As an affiliate marketer, your word is your business which means that if you promote low quality items then your total conversions are likely to drop and will be unlikely to rise again. If you purchase a product and it isn't worth the money, be sure to write about that as well, having negative product reviews as well as positive ones will make the positive reviews you do write more believable.

When using the product, be sure to take plenty of pictures of yourself doing so. Seeing the product in use will make it easier for readers to picture themselves using the product. Each review should include a breakdown of the product describing its pros and cons, but still leaving out a bit of relevant information to ensure that the reader is more likely to click the link you provide (several times throughout the review) to find the information that you left out. Once they are on the purchase page they will be more likely to go ahead and pull the trigger.

Another good option is to talk about the product's strengths but then discuss how it is too complicated for all but the most knowledgeable users, as this will make some users even more likely to purchase it. You will also want to try and create a story around each product, discuss what you were doing while using it and generally give readers as many different ways to connect with the product as possible.

Additionally, it is important to ensure that you market yourself as well as the products you are trying to sell as the more your regular readers feel that you (or a persona you create for this purpose) are an expert in a given field, the greater the weight your reviews will have when they are making up their minds whether or not to purchase a product. The more you go out of the way to make readers relate to you on a personal level, the more they will listen to you when you say that a given product is superior to its competition.

Chapter 5: REITs

If you are interested in the idea of investing in real estate but don't like the idea of dealing with the trouble of finding rental property to purchase, then investing in Real Estate Investment Trusts (REITs) might be more your speed. With this passive income stream, you don't need to worry about having lots of cash already on hand for a large down payment and can get started with virtually any amount. This is because when you invest in REITs you are investing in individual shares the same way you would as if you were investing in a company via buying into their stock. This means, instead of worrying if a given property is ultimately going to turn a profit, all you need to do is choose an REIT that has a proven track record and let their team of analysts make profitable decisions for you. In return for your investment, you will receive dividends just as you would if you invested in dividend producing stocks.

Investing in REITs does have its own drawbacks, however, as it typically requires you to pay taxes on the dividends you receive in addition to paying taxes on the income used to purchase your shares in the first place. If you are hoping to generate passive income as a retirement strategy, however, then you can negate this double taxation by putting the money into an IRA account and agreeing not to touch the funds until you are ready to retire.

REITs were created in the 1960s as a way for the average working individual to partake in the profits generated by larger real estate investments such as hotels and major office complexes, to that end they are required to ensure that 90 percent of their profits return to the shareholders and that more than five individuals control 50 percent of the available shares. Each shareholder then receives an amount of the profits based on the number of shares they hold with no preferential treatment given to those who own more shares. What's more, if you don't like the direction the REIT you have invested in is moving then you are free to sell your shares on the open market at any time with no penalty for doing so. Share prices fluctuate, just like stocks, and you will always have access to the current share price in the moment so you can make the most informed decision possible at any given time.

Types of REITs

There are many different types of REITs to choose from, based around different types of property acquisition. A brief explanation of the pros and cons of each is outlined below.

Residential REITs: The most common type of REIT that you will find focuses on residential properties. They typically invest in apartment complexes with hundreds of units or entire condominium communities rather than individual units. This is the easiest type of REIT to start with, as the basics are easy for even the uninformed to understand. They can make decisions on whether a specific REIT is successful by simply visiting the area where the holdings are located and determining what the competition is like in the area along with how full the current holdings currently are. The general rule is that the emptier space in the holding in question the weaker the REITs position currently is. It is also important to be aware of any new construction that is taking place in the area as additional housing options will hurt the REIT's investments as well.

Retail REITs: These REITs typically specialize in either shopping centers or shopping malls, though the latter is becoming increasingly rare. This is another situation where a little bit of feet-on-the-ground investigation can easily tell you how the holdings are doing, and thus how likely the REIT is to see share prices move in the desired direction. Another good thing about these types of investment is that it is unlikely that they will have to deal with an unexpected influx of new competition as new construction in this sector is relatively sparse and requires a great deal of preplanning which means a look at local town hall meetings should be enough to tell you what to expect.

Industrial and office REITS: These two types of REITs are often grouped together simply because the leasing terms of tenants are typically much longer than with other types of REITs. Additionally, they are both more likely to experience success or failure in the present based on conditions that occurred in the past. If they experienced an influx of new tenants when space was at a premium then they are likely to exceed projections while the current leases are in place. Meanwhile, if there was plenty of space to go around at this time then they are likely to be operating with profit projections that are somewhat more modest.

Hotel and Resort REITs: These types of REITs typically show the greatest amount of profit per share, when they are profitable, though the buy-in is typically going to be the highest of any of the other REIT types as well. They are very rarely going to be subject to unexpected competition because the requirements for building something on this scale are going to require plenty of permits which will give the REIT plenty of notice that things might be changing in the future. The biggest downside to these REITs is that they are the least recession proof of any REIT as this type of expense is the first that many people cut out of their budget when things get tight.

Storage REITs: On the other end of the spectrum you have REITs that focus exclusively on business that sell storage space. They typically have the lowest overall buy-in costs. Additionally, while their dividends are typically going to be lower than most other REITs, they have proven to be extremely reliable regardless of the current state of the economy.

Chapter 6: Retail Arbitrage

If you are interested in selling physical items online and don't want to go to the hassle of opening your own online store then retail arbitrage might be for you. Originally an exclusive to those who traded in the foreign exchange currency market, arbitrage is simply the idea of purchasing a commodity at one price and then selling it elsewhere for a higher price. The rise of online marketplaces means that anyone can participate in retail arbitrage, as long as they are able to purchase items at a price that means they can be resold elsewhere for a profit.

Starting out: The biggest asset when it comes to retail arbitrage is a good nose for a great bargain. Your two biggest assets in this quest are going to be the Amazon Price check app and the eBay seller's application as these two sites are typically going to be the best place to go to sell your items for a profit. Both of these applications will help you determine the baseline price an item is selling for so you can decide if the price you are considering purchasing it at is worth the trouble.

In addition to these free applications, you are also going to want to consider the Profit Bandit application. While it has a $10 up front cost, it provides you with a wide variety of information that the free apps lack. Specifically, it will tell you how the current price of an item stacks up to the price of that item overall and also if the product is being sold by Amazon directly or if it violates their code of conduct and why. It will also tell you how much profit you stand to make off of an item based on the amount you are paying, the amount you will sell it for and any extraneous costs that might be incurred.

Finding the best items: When it comes to finding the right items to sell, many people automatically think of big-ticket items, under the rationale that, if they can be found on sale, then the profit would be substantial. While these types of items will occasionally pan out, you will almost always find a more reliable return on basic items that everyone needs as they will sell faster and more readily be found for a discounted price. While this isn't the most exciting advice, products like batteries, diapers and ink cartridges are always going to be able to ensure that your retail arbitrage business turns a profit.

While they won't necessarily sell right away, a great type of product to consider selling is seasonal items such as Halloween or Christmas decorations. These items can typically be picked up for pennies on the dollar in the days immediately following the holiday and if you are willing to wait almost a year to sell them, will always return a reliable profit, especially if you wait to a week or so before the holiday to post them for sale. The downside with this being you only have a limited window in order to ensure that the item sells or else you have to hold onto it for another entire year.

Another good choice is to keep your ear to the ground when it comes to new trends and then purchase a large amount of the new hot item in bulk before the price catches up to its new level of popularity. For example, these days' kids are all about fidget spinners that have lead the price of many versions of this product to increase dramatically. If you had hopped onto the fidget spinner bandwagon early on, then you could now sell them for a significant profit.

Finally, items from the dollar store that feature popular licensed characters such as Disney princesses or Marvel superheroes are always going to be able to turn a profit. While these products might not sell for much more than their purchase price at the moment, if you wait until a specific product is hard to find, typically four to six months, then you can easily sell it for five times what you paid for it to parents who are desperate for new content for their child who has already consumed everything else with their favorite character's face on the box.

Additional concerns: Outside of just looking for the best deals, you are also going to want to special attention to how a given item is likely to ship before buying in bulk. Keeping this factor in mind will make it easier to prevent a rash of returns on products that are exceedingly fragile or are otherwise difficult or exceedingly costly to ship. Furthermore, you will want to avoid items that are going to be complicated to ship as, if things go well, you will be shipping them out on an exceedingly frequent basis.

With these types of items, a good rule of thumb is to only move forward with sales that will net you at least 50 percent profit on the sold item. The only exception to this rule is if you have a specific idea in mind for the product when you purchase it and don't mind making less from it overall.

eBay to Amazon arbitrage: If you are looking to get into arbitrage without having to purchase any physical products, then you can actually play eBay and Amazon against one another. Specifically, what you do is spend time searching both eBay and Amazon for specific items and then, once you find a product that is selling for more on eBay, simply post a new auction and then, once it ends, purchase the product on Amazon and send it to the winner of the auction as a gift. While Amazon currently frowns upon this, it is not, strictly speaking, breaking any laws.

When it comes to completing this type of arbitrage sale successfully, it is important to ensure that the items you choose aren't on sale on Amazon for an exceedingly limited time as once an auction has been won it is difficult to get out of sending an item, even if you aren't going to make any money for it. Additionally, it is important to always only post a single auction at a time. Not only will this prevent you from losing money if the price changes on Amazon, it will make the buyer more likely to pull the trigger because of the apparent level of scarcity that having only one option provides.

Chapter 7: Webinars

While creating digital content that other people are legitimately interested in purchasing can take more time and cost more money upfront than selling physical products, eventually you will reach a point where the profit is rolling in without having to do nearly as much work. When you factor in the fact that you don't have to deal with shipping or storage costs, it may even be the more profitable option. While creating the content itself doesn't necessarily need to be terribly time consuming, you will need to spend a good deal of time marketing yourself if you hope to be successful in the long run.

Finding the right topic: In order to create a successful webinar, the first thing you will want to do is to determine what hobbies, talents and skills you are intimately familiar enough with to ensure that other people would be willing to hear you talk about them. It is important to be fluent enough in a given topic that you can provide insight greater than what can currently be found on YouTube regarding the topic for free. This means you not only need to know the topic inside and out, you need to be able to clearly and concisely teach it to others as well.

If nothing immediately comes to mind, the first thing you will want to do is to make a list of all your best skills. Almost everyone has something that they are adept at enough in order to generate at least one webinar, these skills can just be hard to see because you do them well without thinking about it. These topics can be anything from general self-help and how-to topics to more specific things that many people often think of as innate skills such as time management or organizational skills. If you are so good at something that you don't think of it right away then this is likely a good candidate for a webinar.

Express your content clearly: With a viable topic in mind, the next thing you are going to need to do is determine the best way to express your topic in a way that makes it easy for other people to follow along. Depending on the topic you choose, this could be something as simple as recording yourself talking about the topic while doing it or it could be more complicated and including some type of PowerPoint presentation. While the exact way you go about explaining your content doesn't matter, it is important that the visual and audio quality is professional, after all you want to come off as an expert in the field, not someone who is trying to make extra money off of a YouTube video recorded on their phone.

Build a website: Once you create your content, it is important that you find a place to put it online that adds to the entire experience. This means you are going to want to do more than simply throw up a link to the video and a link to PayPal, you are also going to need to create free content that makes visitors interested in seeing what's behind the paywall. This means creating plenty of blogs, and even some free videos that show you are knowledgeable on the topic to the point that visitors are willing to trust you enough to pay for your expert level webinar.

If you have never built a website before, there are plenty of options when it comes to creating something that is functional, if not necessarily flashy. While completely free options are available, you are going to want to invest at least enough in your platform so that you can have your own domain as this will help to build your professional brand. Having an official sounding name will go a long way toward legitimizing your content, which will make it more likely that visitors will be willing to pay for it.

Market your content: Once you have a website that is full of content, both paid and free, the next thing you will want to do is get the word out about your webinar. The first thing you are going to want to do is to spread the word via social media and encourage all of your friends and family to do the same; you never know when something might go viral and word of mouth is enough to boost the sales of a webinar significantly if it gets in front of the right people.

With that out of the way, the next thing you will want to do is visit websites that the people in your chosen niche are likely to congregate around. Once you find these sites you are going to want to spend time in their forums, answering questions that people pose about the topics. Every time you do so, you are then going to want to credit your site as the place you found the information. With enough posts all carrying your website you can be sure that word will start to spread and you will start to see additional hits on your primary site as a result.

Finally, it is important that you include the right type of Search Engine Optimization for your site. This means including the right key phrases as well as a well thought out description to help you show up when people search for the topic you are discussing. The right SEO is extremely important which means that if you don't know what you are doing it is worth paying someone else to do it for you, whatever the cost, you are likely to make it back ten-fold from the extra hits you will receive.

Create an email list: As part of your checkout process, it is important to offer users the ability to sign up for your email list so they can be told when new webinars are available. There is no better audience than one that has already purchased your content, which means whenever you create something new, you will want to send out an email letting these folks know that it is available.

Chapter 8: Author an eBook

If you have detailed knowledge of a particular topic, and want to capitalize on that knowledge without being on camera, then writing an eBook is a valid choice. E-books have been outselling traditional books since 20012 and it is extremely easy to capitalize on this fact and get your piece of the pie. What's more, even if you aren't terribly knowledgeable on a topic, or if your writing skills aren't up to snuff, you can find someone to write a book for you through a surprisingly cheap and easy process.

Get your eBook created: First things first, if you aren't interested in putting together your own eBook, then you can visit a labor sourcing website such as UpWork.com to find easy access to thousands of different writers who are all anxious to complete the task for you. All you have to do is to sign up for a free account and post a listing outlining the basics of what you are looking for and the offers will start flooding in. Then it is simply a matter of finding the writer whose style you like the most and agreeing on the price. Assuming the product you are looking for isn't too complicated the average rate for ghostwriters on UpWork.com is $1 per 100 words, which means you can get an average length eBook for about $100.

Once you have the manuscript in hand, you can then visit Fiverr.com and create a profile before finding someone to format your book for the Kindle Marketplace for $5 and then pay another $5 to have someone create a cover. This means that for less than $120, and no work on your part, you can create something that has the potential to continue generating a profit indefinitely.

Post the book to the Kindle Marketplace: Once you have your book in hand, the next step will be to start making money from it. This is as simple as visiting the Kindle Marketplace and submitting the book, as it doesn't cost you anything to add your book to the marketplace. Instead, Amazon takes a percentage of each eBook that is sold and sends you the rest in the form of a biweekly check. Amazon typically takes 70 percent of the total profit for books that are priced anywhere between $2.99 and $9.99. However, they only take 35 percent of books that are priced below $2.99 and above $9.99. This means that if you price your book at the $1.99 price point you will actually make a greater profit than if you price it at the more common $2.99 price point. What's more, this will also lead to a greater increase in sales, as your book will then be seen as a bargain.

The most common books in the Kindle Marketplace are comprised of the self-help and how-to genres as people who are fans of these genres are always looking for fresh takes on existing problems. Even better, they are condition to always be looking for new ways to solve their problems so just by being new to the Marketplace your book will likely see a boost to its sales.

Find the best topic: If you have already created a webinar then this is a great way to supplement that content. You can then either give your book away for free as a value add for people who purchase your webinar, or even to encourage more people to sign up for your email newsletter. You can also offer it for sale on your website as long as the content differs from what you have already created so that your most diehard fans don't feel cheated by paying for the same content twice.

If you are instead going to have someone else write the book for you, your best bet is to choose a topic that is relatively easy to research, while still not being so simple that those who would be interested in purchasing your book don't just go out and do the research themselves. Additionally, once you find a topic you are interested in pursuing, it is important to visit the Kindle Marketplace and see what the competition is like. While it is virtually impossible to find a topic that hasn't yet been covered in some capacity, you are going to want to try and find one that isn't full of new books that are coming out every week in order to give your book a chance to find an audience.

While you are on the site you are also going to want to take a look at the reviews of the top books in the category to see what people like and, more importantly, what they don' like about what is on display. You can then use these talking points, as a guidepost for the writer to ensure that the content you produce is as likely to find a growing audience as possible.

Regardless if you are writing the book yourself or if you are having someone else do the writing for you it is important to take some time and consider who the target audience of your book is going to be. A book that is written for experts in a field is going to be quite different from one that is written for beginners and having a clear idea of whom the book is for will make narrowing down the correct content to include a much easier task. Writing with the target audience in mind will also make it much easier to ensure your book ends up with plenty of 5-star reviews as well. Positive reviews are crucial, as they will make sure your book is more than just a flash in the pan and help to turn it into a bonified hit.

Ensure your cover is eye catching: When browsing Fiverr.com in order to find the right graphic artist for your cover, it is important to keep in mind that roughly 90 percent of all eBook purchases are based on the cover alone. This means you are going to want to have something that looks profession and eye-catching that stands out from the crowd. When placing your request as for something outside the norm or you are likely to end up with a cover that looks like 9 out of 10 on your chosen topic and your sales will suffer because of it.

Chapter 9: Stock Photos

If you are already familiar with what is required to take a great photo, and you have a way to take photos that is more advanced than your smartphone, then taking photos and selling them to stock photo websites can be an easy way to generate a steady stream of passive income.

Getting started: There are several major sites that you can apply to if you are interested in pursuing this type of passive income steam including iStockPhoto.com and ShutterStock.com. Each of these sites allows aspiring photographers to post content to their site in exchange for a percentage of the profits when a third party pays to license a picture. These sites generally take between 50 and 85 percent of the profits from each photo with more experienced photographers getting a larger percent of the profits. What this means is that selling stock photos is a numbers game with a quantity of sales being key to success in the long run.

Understand what sells: The first step towards making money through this type of passive income stream is determining what type of photos customers are looking for and understanding how to reproduce the quality that you find. Assuming you are already familiar with the basics of quality photography that means you are going to want to spend some time looking through various categories of photos you are interested in. You will want to find a category that is active enough to make it worth your while to contribute to it, while not being so stuffed with content that it is going to be difficult to get yourself noticed. You will also want to take note of the photos that seemed to be picked the most so that you can get an idea of what types of pictures those who frequent those sites are looking for.

Take some pictures: After you have a clear idea of the types of pictures you are to take, the next step is to get out there and start taking pictures. It was mentioned before, but it bears repeating, if you want to find success in this passive income stream then you are going to want to use something nicer than your smartphone camera. While those pictures have the potential to be relatively good quality, especially considering where that technology was just a few years ago, if you try and submit smartphone pictures to these sites there is a very high chance that you will be rejected.

Once you have a number of shots that you feel are of the quality required to get your foot in the door, before you submit them you are going to want to go over them with a fine-toothed comb. To do so you are going to want to blow them up to the largest size possible and keep an eye out for small imperfections that might not otherwise be visible. You never know what size photo customers are going to be looking for and you don't want to lose out on a sale just because something isn't right at the largest size. Besides that, you are always going to want to stick to an exposure rate that is set to 100 percent and to also use a tripod, as blurry pictures are almost never going to be accepted unless the blurriness is obviously done for effect.

Submit the photos: The submission process for the major sites is relatively straightforward, you simply choose a few of your best shots and then send them along to be analyzed by a team of professional who work for the site in question. Once you have been accepted you will need to create a profile. Once you have been given access to post new pictures at your own discretion you will want to ensure that each photo you upload features descriptive text that makes it clear what the photo is of as well as a variety of descriptors that will make it more likely to show up in as many different relevant searches as possible.

You will want to include common keywords as well as those that are outside of the box as your idea will sometimes rub potential customers the right way and they will go for it when they otherwise would have picked something more mainstream. This doesn't mean you are going to want to list your photo in every category possible, however, as doing so is only going to cause people to start ignoring your work, even if it comes up in a category that is actually relevant.

If your work doesn't get accepted to the major sites, you may find success with some of the smaller stock photo sites out there that have much less strict application requirements. As almost anyone can be accepted to these sites, if your work is better than average, but just not quite good enough for the major players then you may even find that these sites work in your favor. What's more, they typically pay a larger cut even to new photographers to make up for the fact that they see a fewer number of customers on average. Remember, stock photos are a numbers game so the more places your photos can be seen by the masses the better.

Promote your photos: When posting your photos to the sites you have been accepted to, it is important to not ignore the free photos section. While posting free photos might seem like a bad way to make money, in reality the opposite is true. If customers aren't ready to pay for a photo quite yet, getting your name in the free section is a good way to get them thinking about your work so that when they are ready to purchase your name is already in their mind. Consider this as an advertising cost and you will likely see more productive hits in the long run.

Chapter 10: Instagram

Instagram is currently seeing more than 400 million users on its site every month and nearly one fourth of those visit the site every single day. With numbers like that it isn't hard to see why advertisers are currently looking to capitalize on content creators that have a significant following. While starting an Instagram page now isn't exactly getting in on the ground floor, when it comes to passive income streams it can still be a profitable and fairly open market.

Determine your focus: In order to build the type of audience that advertisers are looking for, the first thing you are going to need to do is focus on generating a loyal following, with the more followers the better. The greater the number of followers you have, the more you will ultimately be able to make via advertising. A good number to shoot for is 20,000 followers before you start reaching out to advertisers and if you reach 100,000 followers then you can currently expect to make anywhere from $5,000 to $10,000 each month in advertising revenue.

The easiest way to start building your number of followers is to add the right types of details to your profile. Information about yourself and the content you post is a good place to start but you are going to want to include plenty more as well. Specifically, you are going to want to include relevant keywords along with popular hashtags as that will help those interested in your chosen niche find you more easily which means you won't just be posting pictures into the ether. It is important that you choose a niche that you are going to remain interested in for a prolonged period of time. If you have a topic in mind but feel you will be bored of it within six months or less it is best to go back to the drawing board as succeeding in this market means interacting with your chosen niche every single day.

Find the right details: In order to ensure you are using keywords and hashtags that are popular, and thus potentially profitable, the first thing you are going to want to do is search Instagram and see how many other users are using the same ones. You aren't going to simply want to use, as may keywords as possible, as this won't get you any new followers, instead you are going to want to stick to those that are actually relevant to the types of pictures you are actually taking. Careful curation is key to attracting niche followers while also not showing up so frequently that searchers consider your page as spam.

Post every single day: Once you have an idea of the type of content you are going to regularly post, it is important to get into the habit of posting multiple times per day, every single day. You will want to find a schedule of posting that you can stick with long enough that potential followers get used to visiting your page every single day and checking in multiple times as well. Once they realize they are visiting your page this often then they will take the plunge and become your followers rather than having to track your page down manually.

It is important to keep in mind that this will only work if you are taking the types of pictures that people are legitimately interested in seeing. If you don't naturally take lots of pictures then you are probably better off pursuing a different passive income stream.

Taking the right types of pictures: In order to determine what types of pictures your potential followers are going to be interested in, you are going to want to visit the pages of plenty of popular individuals in your chosen niche. This doesn't mean you are going to simply want to copy what you find there, however, but instead you are going to want to use what you find as inspiration. This will help get your creative juices flowing and make it easier to come up with content of your own in the future. Developing your own unique perspective is crucial to being successful in the long run.

While you are on these pages, you are going to want to do more than simply lurk, instead you are going to want to post comments on pictures you like and start interacting with the community. After all, running a successful Instagram isn't just about posting photos, it is about being a personality. Then, once people associated with the niche find your page, you won't be just another random person you will be another member of the community.

Tag individual photos: Once you have taken plenty of pictures that you think the community will enjoy, it is important to go ahead and post them using the keywords and hashtags that you find other people using. Additionally, you are going to want to develop your own keyword or hashtag that your followers can associate with all of your pictures. This will help make it easier for them to keep track of all your new posts.

Turn a profit: Once you have built up a sizeable following, you can start strengthening your passive income stream. The easiest way to go about doing so is by posting pictures of yourself with niche specific products and then including a link to those products and explaining where people can purchase them. The Amazon affiliate program is great for this, but only if you don't abuse it. If your page suddenly changes from niche specific photos to nothing but affiliate marketing then your follower count will suffer as a result. Instead, you are going to want to work these types of pictures into your content stream naturally.

Also, you are going to want to look into advertisers that work via the pay per click model. Essentially how it works is that you offer advertising space on your page and then receive a small amount of compensation each time one of your followers clicks on the ad, regardless of what they do after they have done so. While the average rate for this type of advertisement is just a few cents per click, with at least 20,000 followers this can still add up rather quickly. Additionally, you can look for advertisers who pay per impression, which means you get paid every time a follower visits your page, regardless of whether or not they click on anything. The rate for these types of ads is even less than the pay per click model, but a combination of both can be a profitable venture.

Conclusion

Thank you for making it through to the end of Passive Income Stream Generator: Top 10 Ways to Financial Freedom, let's hope it was informative and able to provide you with all of the tools you need to achieve your goals, whatever it is that they may be. Just because you've finished this book doesn't mean there is nothing left to learn on the topic, expanding your horizons is the only way to find the mastery you seek. New types of passive income streams are always being discovered and the only way you will stay on top of them is by doing your own research.

As you can see, there are plenty of different ways to generate passive income, but getting them up and running requires hard work and dedication before you can sit back and reap the rewards from all of your hard work. This means you are going to want to pick one of the types of passive income discussed in the previous chapters and dedicate yourself to it until it starts turning a profit. Flitting from one type of passive income stream to the next will only end up burning you out on the process as a whole without generating any real revenue in the process.

When you are in the midst of setting up a passive income stream it can be easy to lose sight of the end goal amidst the hard work. It is important to stay the course, however, and to keep in mind that the ends are certainly going to justify the means. You don't need anything special in order to set up a successful passive income stream, you just need to commit yourself to the process and see it through to completion. Remember, generating passive income is a marathon, not a sprint; slow and steady wins the race.

Finally, if you found this book useful in anyway, a review on Amazon is always appreciated!

www.ingramcontent.com/pod-product-compliance
Lightning Source LLC
Chambersburg PA
CBHW071241220526
45468CB00002B/953